Ekogo Ekogo

MOB LYNCHING
(Drama)

First Published in 2021

Miraclaire Publishing
Kansas City, MO 64133, USA
www.miraclairepublishing.com / info@miraclairepublishing.com

In association with
Ken Scholars Publishing, USA

>ISBN-13: 978-1-954154-06-3
>© 2021 Miraclaire Publishing

All rights reserved.
No part of this book may be reproduced, stored in a retrieval system, or transmitted, in any form or by any means, electronic, mechanical, photocopying, recording or otherwise, without the prior permission of the copyright owner.

Printed in the United States of America

Miraclaire Publishing makes every effort to ensure the accuracy of all the information ("Content") in its publications. However, Miraclaire and its agents and licensors make no representations or warranties whatsoever as to the accuracy, completeness, or suitability for any purpose of the Content and disclaim all such representations and warranties, whether expressed or implied to the maximum extent permitted by law. Any views expressed in this publication are the views of the author and are not necessarily the views of Miraclaire.

Dramatis Personae

Old man/Mr Tchechu: A shoe trader and father of Nana.
Nana: Mr. Tchechu's son.
Mbella: Mr. Tchechu's Friend
Okerekere: A shoe trader from Nigeria. Mr. Tchechu's neighbour and friend.
An Imbecile
Constable: A police officer in Khaki shorts.
The Mob
Gentleman: A young man of twenty-five years old, dark skin, a blond wavy hair, an aquiline nose and red lips.
Matute: Ndola's friend
Boy: a market rogue
Man: an observer
Mbua: an observer
Limuga: an observer
Woman
Police Woman
Second Police Woman
Inspector Choko Choko
Cripple
Halfarm
Blindman
Madman
Bitterman
Bastard
Passer-by
First Officer
Second Officer

FIRST MOVEMENT

Buea-town market. A shoe shop. Bold caption on the wall above the door: AMERICA WONDER. The owner, Mr. Tchechu, an aged man in his late fifties, has been dozing. He wakes up, yawns with fatigue, stretches, then walks out probably to revive himself when he finds a figure huddled up on the veranda, snoring.

OLD-MAN:
You again here!
You must be sick in the head!
(*Almost immediately, he makes a rush toward the dozing figure and wakes him with a ruthless kick on the buttocks.*) Seed of the devil! Disappear! Vamoose!
(*The imbecile starts up from his slumber, confused; another pungent kick sends him twisting in pain like a snake caught in lit coal. Reality strikes him. As the idiot flees away, the man lands an excruciating blow on his back. His scream is that of a pig under torture.*)
Serves you right! Dirty rotten swine! Vulture head! Has my shop become a nest for you to come and nestle your lice and bedbugs? Come here smearing and polluting my ground with your unbearable stench of bad luck! God punish you! No wonder! Dawn has come with its own portion of bad luck: not even a soul had stopped by for window shopping! Carry that smelly offensive tears and a mouth that drools elsewhere! Son of the devil!
(*He crosses himself three or four times in rapid succession; lifts arms to the sky.*) Lord, loving father, return my ground its purity. Let customers – in thousands – draw near as butterflies to flowers.
(*He enters the shop, goes down on his knees and takes a prayer posture.*)
Blackout.

SECOND MOVEMENT

Minutes later. Rain had fallen. The stinking gutters overflow with dirty brown water. There is a crowd in front of Mr. Tchechu's shop. The people speak all at once, clap hands and frequently exclaim, "Wonders shall never end!" A whistle blows, dead silence. The people make way as a constable dressed in khaki shorts, a baton in his right hand moves on stage. He puts on an intimidating look.

CONSTABLE:
What is this noise?
What is this violation of public tranquillity!

THE MOB:
Er... morning chef ... good morning... it's ...

CONSTABLE:
(Pointing menacingly at a man.) You! ID-card?
(The man, shaken, hurries off stage. A few others join him as well. The officer seems happy with the result. He paces exaggeratedly, and then uses his baton to point at another man in the crowd.) You!

MAN:
(Looking behind him.) Mm...me?

CONSTABLE:
Yes, you. What is happening here?

MAN:
Chef... it is...it is a fight; I mean a quarrel between Papa Tchechu here and that gentleman over there – the man in white.

GENTLEMAN:
(Speaking with an exaggerated American accent.) Pardon me, man. I ain't no trouble maker. Never! This old man disrespects me. He kinda accuses me falsely.

CONSTABLE:
(The officer stares open-mouthed at the gentleman. He is dressed up to the nines. The officer seems lost in admiration. He collects himself and swallows labouriously.)
Mr. Man in white, the old man accuses you of what exactly?

GENTLEMAN:
He accuses me of theft. *(At the mention of "theft", the people regrettably cry out in disbelief and utter astonishment.)*

CONSTABLE:
(Blows into a whistle.) Silence! Silence! If you disrupt my duty one more time, you will sweat blood in cell.
(The officer walks over to the gentleman, walks about him, gazing him with a strange but balance dose of fake intimidation and can't-help-it envy. He switches over to the old man, studies him slowly and steadily from head to toe. He sighs and reaches out his right hand.)
Your ID-card.
(With shaky hands, the old man brings out from his pocket a piece of dirty-brown paper and hands it to the officer. He stammers.) Tche…Tche…Tche..

OLD-MAN:
Tchechu Francois, chef. Tchechu.

CONSTABLE:
Yes, Mr Tchechu, what do you say this white man has stolen from you?

OLD-MAN:
Thank you, chef.

CONSTABLE:
Don't thank me. Answer the question.

OLD-MAN:
Chef, it is a simple story but hard to believe.

CONSTABLE:
Go on, old man. Do your best to convince me – convince me.

OLD-MAN:
God help me. (*Swallows hard.*) This day has been the bleakest ever since I started this trade. It started with the heavy downpour. Then that curse devil! That vampire came snoring at my doorsteps and drove my customers away. I would blame myself had I not prayed this morning, but I did. I did.

CONSTABLE:
I am not interested in your relationship with God, old man. Just stick to the case.

OLD-MAN:
Sorry Chef …I …I was beginning to give up when suddenly I saw the light of God in its entire splendour walk into my shop.

CONSTABLE:
(*Perplexed.*) The light of what?

OLD-MAN:
(*Pointing at the Gentleman.*) I mean this man walked in – the so-called angel; angel from hell. Yes, demon in white robes! Everything on him was white: a white hat, a white three-piece suit, a white shirt, a white brief-case. Everything white and sparkling except one: his shoes.

CONSTABLE:
(*All the more baffled.*) His shoes?

OLD-Man:
In fact, he was not wearing shoes.

CONSTABLE:
(*Looks at the Gentleman's shoes, then at the old man.*) Wait! You mean…you mean the man in white walked in here in bare feet?

OLD-MAN:
As a matter of fact, he was wearing a pair of battered old sandals when he stepped into my shop. (*There is a roar from unbelievers. The whistle brings them to order.*)

CONSTABLE:
(*The officer directs a stare of complete disbelief toward the old man.*) Now what is this confusion, old man? First, the man in white was not wearing shoes and then he was wearing sandals. What do you want me to believe?

OLD-MAN:
Shoes are shoes and sandals are sandals. One is not the other.

CONSTABLE:
Come, come old man, what is this logic? (*Pauses.*) Well, since you talk logic and fact, bring out the fact, bring out the battered sandals.

OLD-MAN:
That is what I was trying to explain... (*Swallows hard.*) The very moment I set eyes on the man in white I said to myself, "My day is blessed. Here comes a big fish. Let me seek for a big net and an attractive bait." I had but one pair that befitted his calibre: a fine snow-white pair of loafers, probably now brown with dust under one of the *Ghana-must-go bags*. In all haste, I set to digging – digging and digging into the bags, one after another: the first one, the second, and then the third – then I found it. Not a speck of dust anywhere. I showed it to the man and said, "Nice pair." So, I fitted the pair into his feet and said, "Ah! A Turtle in its shell." The man turned his feet this way and that, admiring the cute pair. He tried three or four steps, to and fro, to relish the comfort of the shoe under his feet. And then he searched into the sparkling snow-white brief-case and brought out a wad of fine smelly shiny new notes. He said, "How much?" I said, "Only ninety-five." He didn't argue, neither did he pay me. Counted the notes and then said, "Can I have a nylon bag?" I said, "Naturally." I handed him a black plastic bag with the inscription "AMERICA WONDER" He leant forward, picked up his stinking scattered old sandals as if a pile of shit, threw it into the plastic bag, fastened it and then walked outside and dropped the bag, with a crafty and pretentious accidental gesture, into the fast flowing gutter. In no time, the rain-water bore the plastic-bag to God-knows-where. He then returned to the shop, kept the money away into the brief-case, then turned round and said with a smile on his face, "Thank you, Mr.

AMERICA WONDER." I said, "You're welcome sah, but my money." He said, "What money?" I said, "Money for the pair." He said, "What pair? What are you talking about?" I said, "What is this nonsense?" He said, "Listen and listen well, old man. I don't know you, have never seen you." I said, "Bloody devil!" And then I jumped on him and then came the crowd and you after.

CONSTABLE:
(Looks at the man in white then at the old man. The gesture is repeated in rapid succession and then he bursts into a can't-help-it laughter. The crowd laughs with him. He abruptly stops. The mob Silences. He frowns. Gathers himself together and feigns seriousness.)
This is hard to believe, old man. Why would this fine gentleman readily take out sweet smelling notes from his splendid snow-white brief-case and then put them back without paying you?

OLD-MAN:
Put the question to him.

CONSTABLE:
(Shouting.) No! You answer the question, old man. Answer!

OLD-MAN:
I ... I don't know...my only worry is my pair or my money. He won't walk away with both or else...

CONSTABLE:
(Angrily.) Come come come blessed Jesus! You have the guts to threaten an authority of my rank?

OLD-MAN:
My money or my shoes, chef...my money or...

CONSTABLE:
Silence old man! Shut up before I blow your brains. Do not forget that I have the last word in this matter; and my final word cannot be refuted. Well, let me tell you what I think about this matter. *(Coughs to clear his throat.)* Considering my long-standing and indisputably rich and outstanding three-month career of a police officer, I tell you without fear nor doubt that hurricanes and volcanoes have come my way but I have stood up to them all. I am the only officer who had managed to drag a confession out of petty thieves and criminals before they are burnt alive. How many never-do-well idiots have I brutalized into accepting pregnancy they are not responsible for? And if your mango, guava, pawpaw or whatever tree has been robbed, just beep me. I will come with my Kalashnikov and baton and the boys in that vicinity shall weep and confess – I don't care whether they are guilty or not. I don't mean to blow my own trumpet, but there is no case too big or too small for me. I trash everything on my way. My judgment is acute. And mark you, I am never wrong. Never! *(The officer paces in silence, playing with the baton.)* Now old man, this is what I think: If you say the pair of white loafer comes from your shop, then it only seems right that you claim the white hat, the white suit, the white shirt, the white tie, the white brief-case and the white everything. Can you not see that it is a collection, or are you blind?

OLD-MAN:
But Chef, you would avoid a clumsy conclusion if you don't make generalisa…

CONSTABLE:
Shut up your mouth and listen! We have had enough of your silly tale! *(He moves toward the gentleman.)* Pardon

my curiosity gentleman but I must know: did you actually set foot in AMERICA WONDER?

GENTLEMAN:
Actually, I did officer but not to make a purchase. The site simply doesn't kinda suit my taste.

CONSTABLE:
(*Excitedly.*) Eh heh, good! Good! (*Feigns seriousness.*) But then, what was your business there?

GENTLEMAN:
Actually, I'd come here to kinda check on somebody – an old bud. Days back before I travelled to the States, he kinda owned a fruit stall along this line.

CONSTABLE:
(*Excited.*) Yes, yes, yes. You are very very right. That is before the new market was built.

GENTLEMAN:
(*Nods elegantly and with extra-confidence.*) And ever since my stay in the States I had kinda lost every God-damn contact with my buddy. Now that I'm back home I said to myself, "Why don't you go seek your buddy and kinda get things fixed back?"

CONSTABLE:
I see. So, what is the name of the lucky one?

GENTLEMAN:
(*Confused.*) Who?

GENTLEMAN:
(*Enthusiastically.*) The friend you are looking for.

GENTLEMAN:
Oh! Ndola…He is called Ndola.

MATUTE:
(Breaks in.) Did you say Ndola? Ndola Niba? I know him.

GENTLEMAN:
You do? How do I get his contact?

MATUTE:
Well, I can't say. He travelled abroad – to Germany.

GENTLEMAN:
Now I kinda understand the line that never went through. I thought his line was jammed but it was blocked. *(Pause.)* And the strange lot of faces I had seen in his dwelling!

MATUTE:
His mother passed away and his father sold up his home and returned to his village.

GENTLEMAN:
Damn! Damn!

CONSTABLE:
Sorry'o white man. Take heart. Life is strange. *(Suddenly gives out a long dry laugh.)* You see, I like the way you talk, like Clinton, Bush, Obama…damp! Shirt-men! Are you American or Cameroonian?

GENTLEMAN:
Well, Kinda America and Cameroon in one.

CONSTABLE:
(Animatedly.) You see! Beautiful accent! Wonderful voice! Sweet short words. Two in one. See, Mr. White man, my own older sister from one womb, I say the same blood flows in our veins has been in Texas America for fifteen years and above now. She has never sent one single *lie-lie* dollar back home but does it matter? Christ Jesus! If you hear her children talk. My nephews twitter like weaver birds. *(Imitating his nephews.)* "I'm gonna break up your damn old neck!"

OLD-MAN:
(Cuts in.) Chef…what are you…

CONSTABLE:
(Deeply engrossed.) "I'm gonna blow out your damn brains!"

OLD-MAN:
Chef!

CONSTABLE:
"I'm gonna knock your damn old ass to hell!"

OLD-MAN:
Chef!

CONSTABLE:
"I'm gonna… *(The officer pulls himself together.)*

OLD-MAN:
What are you doing, chef?

CONSTABLE:
(Visibly angry.) Shut up and don't tell me how to go about my own job! Just shut it up!   *(Faces the gentleman.*

Takes on a serious look.) Your suit, this fine collection – where did you buy it?

GENTLEMAN:
The States no doubt. Where else! The famous world-class and universal stylist J.M.H.D. Bretton Woods kinda have the sole magic fingers to weave such wonder. It is very obvious I kinda own a closet crammed full of such wonder in every possible form and colour you may fancy. Kinda see what I mean?

CONSTABLE:
Certainly, gentleman, certainly. No more questions from me. The issue is clear. *(Turns reluctantly to the Crowd.)* If anyone has something to say, say it now or never. *(He paces about.)*
Yes, *(pointing)* you. Speak.

BOY:
Chef, I was playing a game of cards with my…

CONSTABLE:
(Loudly.) A game of what!

BOY:
(Frightened.) I swear it was not gambling, Chef. We were only killing time.

CONSTABLE:
Good for you. Go on.

BOY:
We were playing when a Mercedes came beaming like streetlamps and then it stopped and then the door opened and then the man in white stepped out and then the door closed and then it drove off and then the man in white

walked to the corridor of shoe-shops and then he disappeared and then two were fighting and then we came and then you came…and then…

CONSTABLE:
(Butts in.) Enough! The truth lies in the shoes. Did you take a look at his shoes?

BOY:
(Uncertain) …yes

CONSTABLE:
Good boy. What colour?

BOY:
I…I…I did not really pay attention to…

CONSTABLE:
(Angrily.) You stupid idiot! Useless goat! Out of my sight!

MBUA:
(Breaks in.) May I say something, chef?

CONSTABLE:
Go ahead. Speak your mind.

MBUA:
Is it not fishy that a befitting king like this white man will wander about in battered old sandals?

CONSTABLE:
(Eagerly.) O-ho! It is even so, my brother. Who can believe such accusations!

LIMUGA:
(Cuts in.) It is true, chef. But we must not doubt that there are snakes in sheep skin, demons in angelic…

CONSTABLE:
Shut off before I cut off your long tongue! Who gave you the go-ahead to air your views in my court?

MBELLA:
(Breaks in.) Chef?

CONTABLE:
Yes, anything to add?

MBELLA:
Yes, ah get small talk, Chef.

CONSTABLE:
(Warningly.) And I will not tolerate any foolishness! Not anymore! Go ahead.

MBELLA:
Ah be na Pa'a Mbella, chef. Pa'a Tchechu na ma friend, very good friend. Ah know Pa'a Tchechu for close to tarty years now, na good and honest man. But again, na hard thing for believe say dis fine white man for wa before na snake, na wayo. Make Ah tell you solution for this trouble, Chef.

CONSTABLE:
Tell me pa'a, tell me quick.

MBELLA:
Make we do proper checking, Chef. Make we go deep down. If dis white man be proper proper for inside then he be proper proper for outside.

CONSTABLE:
(Bemused.) And what do you mean by proper proper?

MBELLA:
If dis man be clean clean inside , dat mean say if singlet na white, knickers na white, socks na white and everything under na white white, then I bet you say everything ontop must be white too. Why nah, na common white shoe go pass he?

CONSTABLE:
(A moment's thought.) Well, old man, you are not wholly stupid. You make some sense. We shall give it a try but before we…yes, *(pointing)* you – you have anything to say?

OKEREKERE:
Oga chef, we thank God' o!

CONSTABLE:
I am listening.

OKEREKERE:
I am "OKEREKERE ALL MODEL" and Pa'a Tchechu is "AMERICA WONDER." I and he we are shoe-trader colleague. We know ourselves for plenty years now. My papa did dis business. He papa did dis business. My papa pass me the business. He papa pass he the business. Oga Chef, in fact, weti I want tell you be dis: Tchechu is hardworking, Tchechu is brave, Tchechu is God-fearing, Tchechu is honest, Tchechu is…

CONSTABLE:
Hold it there! I am sick of this sentimental show-off. Spare me the sermon and go straight to the point.

OKEREKERE:
No vex nah, no vex oga chef. Na say I deh confuse. Everything deh up-side-down inside my head. I no understand.

CONSTABLE:
What don't you understand?

OKEREKERE:
One director son come my shop for purchase a pair of loafers three markets ago. I tell am say I no get expensive shoes. Even Tchechu AMERICA WONDER no get because we vow say we no sell high-class shoes anymore. People too poor to buy. But weti surprise me be say, my brother AMERICA WONDER say dis white man don tief he pair of loafer. Chineke God! How come! Where the loafer comot?

CONSTABLE:
(Excitedly.) Good question. Where the loafer comot? Where, Old man? *(The old man is quiet.)*
Ha! You have lost your tongue!

OLD-MAN:
(Stammers.) Err…no, yes…I remember now. I remember the day you came with that director's son in my shop, but what I told you was a lie.

OKEREKERE:
|Chineke! A lie?

CONSTABLE:
How can we be sure this is not another lie? *(Laughs exaggeratedly.)*

OLD-MAN:
Listen, I am a shoe-trader – a business man. I cannot possibly say the truth all the time. Sometimes I feel obliged to tell a lie and save my business. After all, it is never a bad lie.

CONSTABLE:
Whatever you mean by that! A lie is a lie and it is always bad – very bad. Your best friend and faithful colleague strongly affirm you had no such pair in your shop, but you obstinately charge the gentle man here with stealing your loafer. Mary mother of Jesus! Even the blind can see clear in this case.

OLD-MAN:
It is only a misunderstanding, chef. Permit me explain.

CONSTABLE:
Yes, that is your forte! Explaining explanations of explanations. I am sick and tired of this nonsense.

OLD-MAN:
Chef …please listen. I buy shoes at the Lagos market and resell them at the Buea-town market. The faster they sell, the more turn-over and profit I make. But recently I noticed that costly and high-class shoes are no good for business. The sumptuous pairs catch mould on the shelf as customers would only stop to admire, grin wryly at the price and walk away. And so, I vowed, along with my friend OKEREKERE ALL MODEL not to sell anymore of the luxurious pair to the struggling populace. But chef, no more than a year after the vow, Justice Ayuk Besong walked majestically into my shop and placed an order for a white pair of loafers. Good God I tried to explain, oh yes, I argued, I contested but he shut my mouth off with

an advance of 50000FCFA and was very much ready to pay a balance of 50000FCFA on delivery. I took the money; for am I not a business man?

THE CROWD:
Of course, you are…. it is you right. *(The officer silences them with his whistle.)*

OLD-MAN:
I travelled to Nigeria and stayed in Lagos for a week. On my return to Cameroon, with the goods still on my head, I was taken aback by the news of Justice Ayuk Besong's passing away. Now there was I, a pair of loafers in hand that belonged partly to a dead man and partly to me. But I looked up to my Mighty God, for there is nothing He cannot solve. The solution came in a flash: I visited the bereaved and explained everything to the eldest son. Of course, he promised to settle up with me and claim the pair but he never showed up. *(Pause for a while.)* It was during that very uncertain hour that my friend OKEREKERE ALL MODEL came with a director's son to my shop, wondering whether by some outside chance my old stock of loafers was not sold out. What could I tell him? Could I possibly say "yes" and sell a pair partly mine and partly the dead? No! No! Patience! I didn't give up. A hundred times I paid the eldest son a visit but it seemed he had vanished from this earth. Two years went down the drain and then my mind was made to sell off the shoes; even so, doubt and uncertainty held me back. But today…yes today, the temptation was even bigger and irresistible when I saw the so-called man in white step into my shop. I was thinking I will make a sale after all – only to find out that he is a bunch of rotten bones in a three-piece suit.

GENTLEMAN:
(Angrily.) Better watch your tongue, old man. You kinda disrespect me one more time and I charge you with defamation.

CONSTABLE:
Go ahead and insult. Insult! Whoever gives you the right! *(Brief pause.)* Monkey!
(To the man in white.) Gentleman, you have the right to charge him with defamation of character. Our office is not far – just a stone's throw. Come and pay a small fee and I will do the rest. *(To the old man.)* And you, just wait and see. Your age gives me no pity. Law is law and I stand for law and order. Drop this fake accusation and make light your fine, but you won't hear! When I would've given you twenty-four on your back, buttocks and soles, you would scream and scream but then I would be interested in the truth no more.

OLD-MAN:
(Stands at attention.) If the man in white is not a thief, then I must be mad; I know am not mad.

CONSTABLE:
Fool yourself; not me! Trust me, I will beat this madness out of your old brains. Now without further ado, follow me to the station.
(At this hour, Nana gets onstage. A young and energetic fellow. A bewildered look on his face.)

NANA:
What is this mob outside my shop?
(He spots the old man.) Father?
(He spots the officer.) Ah! Good evening chef.

CONSTABLE:
(Pointing.) Is this man your father?

NANA:
Is anything the matter, chef?

CONSTABLE:
Are you his son?

NANA:
Err… of course. He's my father.

CONSTABLE:
And did I hear you claim this shoe-shop your own?

NANA:
Yes…no…I mean it is my father's and somewhat belongs to me.

CONSTABLE:
Naturally. Well, let me inform you that your father is charged with three offences: (1) False accusation, (2) Character defamation and above all (3) Disruption of public tranquillity.

NANA:
I'm afraid I don't follow you, chef.

CONSTABLE:
Your father here – all grey, staggering, weary, and wretched – charges the man in white there – young, vigorous, steady and wealthy – with stealing a pair of loafers from his shop.

NANA:
(Astonished.) Father!

CONSTABLE:
He claims the gentleman has measured the pair and now refuses to pay for it.

NANA:
God forbid!

CONSTABLE:
He calls the gentleman a crook, a rogue, a thief, a vagabond…in fact, all sorts of heinous names fall on the poor gentleman like thunder rain.

OLD-MAN:
(Stands at attention.) If he is not a crook, then I am mad. I know I am not mad!

NANA:
(Mouth falls open.) Father! You are sick. Haven't we had our fill of trouble?

CONSTABLE:
Oho! It is coming out. The man has been troublesome all through.
(In an attempt to stop his father from speaking, Nana makes for him, but he does not cease to harp on the "thief and mad" slogan. Defeated, Nana hastens towards the officer.)

NANA:
Please chef, please forgive my father. I beg you to have pity on the old man. We are only poor people trying to manage life the best we can.

CONSTABLE:
And so you must insult well-groomed and well-heeled citizens in your struggle for a better life?

NANA:
Chef, the man is old, tired and sick.

CONSTABLE:
Sick?

NANA:
It is clear he has lost his mind. Most of the time he's talking to himself. Talking trash.

OLD-MAN
(Stands at attention.) Either I am mad or he is a thief; I am not mad.

NANA:
(Almost lamenting.) Did I not tell you, Chef? One or two knots have gone loose in his brains. Only yesterday, he couldn't place my aunt, his loving blood-sister. Today I overheard him quarrelling with his father – a man dead and buried for ages now.
(Seeing that the officer is silent, he makes for the man in white, pleading.)
Please sir, pay him no attention. The man is not sound upstairs. Forgive and forget his foolish talk. Does any here doubt the falsity and insanity of his words? Who among the whole lot of shoe-traders is without knowledge of our resolution not to sell anymore prestigious and high-priced shoes the likes of brogues, loafers…?

OLD-MAN:
Foolish ignorant boy! You come and go again and again like the migratory swallow. You cannot be sure of

yourself. You cannot be wholly sure about the nest I have woven and lived in all my life.

NANA:
Do you hear him now? He picks a quarrel with everyone and natters about swallows and nests. It is not the cold clammy cell but rather the warm hospital blanket that will restore him his senses. Sir, I beg of you.

GENTLEMAN:
It's alright. It's ok. I kinda see what you mean; for who does not have a dad? Poor old man. It's fine.

NANA:
God bless you, God bless you, sir.

CONSTABLE:
(Coughs disapprovingly.) I am a man of law and order. Law and order must have its way. The man in white may withdraw his charges, but I – the law – must make sure that the law is respected for the good of the people and society; otherwise, I turn this beautiful and orderly nation into a banana republic. (Brief pause.) Whatever the case, the old man is guilty. We may blame it on age and or neglect but the fact remains – the old man is guilty and liable to fines.

OLD-MAN:
(Stands at attention.) Either I am mad or he is a thief; I am not mad.

CONSTABLE:
Mr. Tch Tchechu Francois, you must go with me to the station. Now!

OLD-MAN:
(Agitatedly)...I am not mad I am not mad I am not mad not mad...
(All of a sudden, he starts like a wild bull and bumps into the gentleman. Shouting "I am not mad" all the time, he does not let go of him. The officer, Nana and some onlookers have a hard time to get him off the gentleman.)

CONSTABLE:
(Sweating profusely from the effort.) Ahah! I see that you are a mad monkey. Trust me, I will beat discipline into your old strong head until it swells and bursts like a useless balloon.

GENTLEMAN:
(Spits.) I have no pity left for him! *(Commanding.)* Officer?

CONSTABLE:
(Snaps to attention.) My colonel, my white man, I mean sir...

GENTLEMAN:
Take this wretch away and see that he regrets for having soiled my suit.

CONSTABLE:
Your wish is my command, sir. *(He shoves the old man forward.)* Move! Move on, old fool! You want the hard way, eh? Ok'oo!
(The old man, whining the "I am not mad" slogan all the time, unexpectedly fights back. He seizes the officer, and they lock in conflict like two rams.)

NANA:
(Lamenting.) I am finished! I am dead! Chef! Father! Chef! Father! Sir! Father!

CONSTABLE:
You challenge authority, eh!

NANA:
Father!

CONSTABLE:
You lay hands on the law in person, eh!

NANA:
Chef!

CONSTABLE:
You are a corpse!

NANA:
Sir! Chef! Chef!

OLD-MAN:
I am not mad...I am not mad...my money or my shoes...I am not mad...I am not mad...no ...no...nomad...my money or my shoes...

NANA:
(The situation is out of hand.)
Chef, please...father, stop this nonsense...please sir forgive and forget...father, Chef...God ...

(Locked in a wrestle, the two men struggle on stage, whirling round and round. Suddenly, a figure emerges from the left flank. Just then, the fighters loosen their grip and, along with the onlookers, make for the far-right flank

of the stage. Noses wrinkle and faces twist in disgust. The crowd swings round to discover the market idiot. On the instant, they sigh disgustingly and carry hands to nostrils. The idiot's rags drip with a blackish-brown watery substance as though from swimming in a pool of vomit. In his hand a black plastic bag that dribbles as well.)

CONSTABLE:
Another fool in my way!

(In the course of escaping the idiot's unbearable stench, the man in white had mistakenly dropped his brief-case in the centre of the stage. Now he comes for it; so that, he is face to face with the idiot, only a few metres apart. They gaze at each other like antagonists. The idiot takes a forward step; the man steps backwards. The idiot then puts out the hand grasping the black plastic bag to the gentleman as though to hand him it. The gentleman is indifferent. Without warning, the idiot flings the bag with an unpredictable exactness that compels the gentleman to catch it and save his suit another smear. In vain. The gentleman looks around angrily and then flings the bag in return to the idiot. The spectacle is funny yet shocking. They cease not to fling the bag at each other until a whistle blows and the officer comes between them. The officer's eyes go from the gentleman and settle on the idiot. The idiot, foaming at the mouth, has recourse to sign language and strives to explain that the gentleman had dropped his bag by accident in the gushing gutters and he (the idiot) had saved it. The officer is quick to adopt the sign language and demands that the idiot throws the bag to him. He does. Slowly, the officer unfastens the bag and holds it up so all can see. He reads the inscription on the bag at full volume, stressing every syllable.) A-ME-RI-CA WON-DER

(The people throw up their hands. The officer proceeds with emptying the content of the bag. A pair of battered old sandals drops on the ground. The onlookers shout all the more in dismay. The officer slowly but steadily fixes a hostile glare at the gentleman. In a flash, the gentleman rams into the officer, shoving him to the ground and disappears in a corner. The officer struggles on his feet, blows his whistle and shouts fiercely.)
Get that man! Catch the thief! Don't let him go! Get him!

(The officer and the onlookers run after the thief, leaving the old man and the idiot (who seems all the more lost and frightened) on stage. The old man stares at the idiot with pity and remorse. His face broadens into a smile; he beckons him to come and inquires in sign language whether he is hungry. The idiot, though astounded by this new and strange experience, readily and continuously nods his head with something of excitement and fear. The old man slowly walks into his shop.)

Blackout

THIRD MOVEMENT

Minutes later. Stage divided into two. A chair and a table at the left side. A phone on the table. On the wall behind the chair is written in bold: POLICE IS YOUR FRIEND. An officer readily fondles a girlish figure. They speak in silent voices, smiling and bursting into shrieks of laughter, and then leave.

A well-furnished parlour at the right side of the stage. On the wall a gigantic portrait of a young man in U.S. Marine uniform cannot be overlooked. The four walls of the house are covered in black and thick tapestry as of a funeral home. The four bulbs, one at each corner, glow no more than candles.

Outside, there is a bang as of a man's heavy fall to the ground. The gentleman enters through the open window, breathing heavily. From all indications he had escaped torture. Except for a once white short, now brown with the passing time, he is naked. His body is smeared with mud, blood and sweat. Footfalls are heard from outside, he hides himself behind the window shade. A woman appears at the room door and makes for the parlour door. The door is bolted. She is shrouded in black from the scarf to the slippers on her feet. From his hideout, the gentleman makes a noiseless leap and seizes the woman by the throat, from behind.

GENTLEMAN:
You cough I strangle! *(Glances around the room.)* Anybody else home? *(The woman can hardly speak, and so shakes her head sideward. The gentleman softens his grip.)*
Listen Ma'a and listen carefully. I am a hardened criminal of the highest order. With my bare hands I have wrung the necks of countless khaki-men, their pistols wasting in

their holsters. Now if you cherish your precious life, just do as I say. *(Shouting.)* Understood?
(The woman nods.) Where is your phone? *(The woman points to the table. He lets go of her.)*
We must call the police. Make haste, call the police.
(She hurries to the phone and begins to dial the number.)
Tell them it's urgent. The devil has a hold over the mob out there. They carry sticks, machetes, iron rods, stones, match-boxes and petrol....Until they set your...your son ablaze they will not rest.

WOMAN:
(Looks up.) My son?

GENTLEMAN:
(Ignores her question.) Tell them your son is innocent. He is not a thief. Has never been. They mistake him for another. Plead with them to make haste or else...
(A police woman gets on the left side of the stage, a file in her hand.)

POLICE WOMAN:
(Calling.) Mr. Chopdoc? Mr. Chopdoc? (Realises she is alone, sighs.) Na whu side dis man go again nah? Na which kind man be dis waka pass dog? E buttocks di scratch for remain one place? One minute, Jezebel enter, they go; another minute, Nalova enter, they go; another one, Bessem enter, they go. Na which kind man dis e no di tire! AhAh! I pity na madame for house'oo! Yi too go nag chest say e get masa. Rubbish! E get sense but no common sense. Me I no go school but I get plenty common sense. No man no fit play me like ball. After all, I get my matriculation; my matricule whey my uncle give me.
(The phone rings. She hesitates, stares at it as if being disturbed. She picks it up.) Hello! Na who be dat?

WOMAN:
(Ardently and hastily.) Good morning madame. Please I am in a terrible horrible situation.　My son is about to be beaten up and burnt to death by a pack of criminals and murderers who accuse –

POLICE WOMAN:
(Cuts in.) Hush! Hush! You want buss my ear? Which kind woman dis tock pass parrot!

WOMAN:
It is a matter of life and death madame. Without rapid intervention from the police, the crowd will set the boy on fire.

POLICE WOMAN:
The crowd? I say eh, weti dis boy do?

WOMAN:
They falsely accuse him of theft.

POLICE WOMAN:
Oho! So na tiefman?

WOMAN:
Falsely accused I said.

POLICE WOMAN:
Weti you mean by *falsely accuse?* Crowd di lie eh? One man get sense pass crowd? Madame, if you no fit accept the simple trut den I no go fit helep you.

WOMAN:
(Softly and slowly.) Madame, this is a serious case. Every passing second is crucial. Rather than tussling over who started the fire, let's strive to put it out first.

POLICE WOMAN:
Faya don do weti?

WOMAN:
(Angrily.) I said let's forget about the petty thieving for now and drag the boy from the savage hands of the mob.

POLICE WOMAN:
Den accept openly sey the boy na tief man. Dat na first step.

WOMAN:
Ok! Alright! Have it your own way. The boy na thief.

POLICE WOMAN:
Eh heh! Na so. You tink sey crowd di craze?

WOMAN:
(Avidly and hurriedly.) Please madame, we really don't have time for this; we are badly in want of a pushback from the police.

POLICE WOMAN:
Sofly madame! Sofly! You see, na so wuna dey spoil pickin dem. Dis kind way you tock non-stop like parrot, you tink sey som tin go enter pickin e head?

WOMAN:
There is really no time for this trashy talk madame. Just send your boys to…

POLICE WOMAN:
Jesus! You call me trash? Me, government authority? So na so? You beg for help and you call me trash? Ok! Save yourself! *(She hangs up.)*

WOMAN:
Hello? Hello? Hello?

POLICE WOMAN:
Idiot! *(She sighs and walks off stage cursing and shaking her huge backside.)*

WOMAN:
She has hung up. Terrible! Terrible! Let me try Buea Centre. *(She opens a directory on the table, flips through the pages, dials a different number and waits. The phone rings. A second police woman walks up to the table and picks up the phone.)*

SECOND POLICE WOMAN:
Bonjour. *(A strong French accent.)* Buea Centrale Police. En quoi puis vous être utile?

WOMAN:
(Stares strangely at the phone.) Good morning madam.

SECOND POLICE WOMAN:
Mooning.

WOMAN:
I am an inhabitant of Buea at the Chief's Street. There is an unruly mob at my door striving to break in, get hold of my son, torture and lynch him. Please, save us. My boy is innocent. He is not a thief. *(Long pause.)* Hello? *(Takes the phone off her ear, looks at it and replaces it on her ear.)* Hello? Hello?

SECOND POLICE WOMAN:
Sori Madame. Je n'ai rien compris.

WOMAN:
(Angrily.) I say my yard is circled by a pack of barbarians who seek to reduce my son to ashes because of a false petty thieving and all you can say is *sorry*?

SECOND POLICE WOMAN :
Calmez-vous, madame. Parlez-vous un peu Français?

WOMAN:
What! I don't understand you! What do you mean? I am a Cameroonian… see, people want to kill my son and, you, the police should come and stop them…that is your duty…

SECOND POLICE WOMAN:
Franchement, je ne comprends rien. Patientez, mon collègue, Mola va venir d'un moment à l'autre…il est toujours en retard…

WOMAN:
(Sighs and hangs up.) How can she? She has no right. No sense of duty. She is supposed to speak some English. We are in Buea.

SECOND POLICE WOMAN:
Allô ? Madame ? Elle a raccroché. Vous aussi, apprenez à parler d'autres langues. En fait, le Cameroun est bilingue. En plus, on ne sait jamais…et le Français est très important au Cameroun…C'est un droit et un devoir…maintenant qui perd alors ? *(She sighs and walks off.)*

WOMAN:
Let me try Molyko. It's far but we never know from where help might come. *(She flips through the directory and dials a third number. The phone rings for a long time.*

A short police man with a bulging stomach enters. He eats "soya" from a brown piece of paper much in the manner of a greedy pig: as though to finish it off before a colleague comes in to share with him. He is in no haste except in masticating. Takes time to walk to the table, pull the chair, sit down, arrange two or three articles on the table. Places his "soya" in the middle of the table like some prestigious trophy, say a gold medal won in some Olympic competition. He is about to answer the call when his mobile phone rings. He searches in his pocket and brings it out, looks at the screen then sighs and frowns. The phone on his table continues to ring. He picks up the call from his mobile phone.)

POLICE MAN:
Yes, what is it again? I hate to be disturbed at my work! *(Brief pause. He listens.)* See, I am sick and tired of your complaints…when will you ever have a franc for yourself? See, what is the use of your orange trade? You just waist time and energy…It's strange that you always have money to call and insult me but never for food. *(Brief pause. Listens.)* Yes, yes, *(He picks a piece from the paper and throws into his mouth and chews violently as if to soothe himself of some internal pressure.)* and what do you want me to do right now? See, nature is a blessing. God is not a fool. Get some leaves, cassava leaves or whatsoever I don't care but the children must not go hungry. *(Brief pause.)* What do you say! Look, be careful woman! You spoil them. When I was a child, I ate cassava leaves every blessed day and I did not die; rather I grew healthier and stronger. *(Brief pause. Licking and sucking his oily fingers.)* I will see what I can do but I promise nothing, and don't expect anything… *(Picks another slice from the paper and throws in mouth.)* I am looking forward to be dispatched to the highway and our troubles will be over. Hello? Are you there? *(He places*

the mobile phone on the table and throws a handful of roast meat in his mouth as if to make up for the lost time. All of a sudden, his mobile phone begins to ring. He is visibly angry and his frown only changes into a broad smile when he gazes at the screen of his phone. He stops the office phone and answers his mobile phone.) Hello, my sweet darling angelic baby... how are you today? Beautiful. *(Listens.)* Hello? *(Takes the phone off his ear, looks at it.)* Hello? No. *(He calls back.)* Hello pretty angel. How can you be angry with me? It pains my heart. I bleed profusely. No, don't say that again. See, I already have three quarter of your money in my drawer ...yes, I have three hundred thousand right now as I am talking to you. *(Listens.)* Yes, you may come for it. *(Listens then laughs)* What? I have eaten nothing. Right now, I am chewing some roast meat. I wish you were here to share with me. Oh! You are coming? Ok, make haste. I will give you a treat my beautiful, pretty, darling, angelic baby girl...shortly shortly... *(He drops the call and laughs for a long time.)* Baby baby... *(The office phone begins to ring again and, now a happy man, he picks it up.)* Police Molyko. Police Inspector Mr. Sako Choko choko. What can I do for you?

WOMAN:
Thank God. Good morning, sir.

INSPECTOR CHOKO CHOKO:
Morning, madame.

WOMAN:
Sir, I beg of you, make haste or you will not save the situation. There is a lynch mob at my gate, threatening to break it down. They mistake my son for a thief and won't budge but roast him alive. Please sir, come quickly before it gets out of hand.

INSPECTOR CHOKO CHOKO:
Calm down, madame. Now what is your name?

WOMAN:
Monjowa Samaritana.

INSPECTOR CHOKO CHOKO:
Where do you live?

WOMAN:
Buea Town, Chief's Street. The place is not hard to find. It is crowded all over.

INSPECTOR CHOKO CHOKO:
What did the boy steal?

WOMAN:
I beg your pardon?

INSPECTOR CHOKO CHOKO:
I said what did he steal?

WOMAN:
I said he didn't steal any…

GENTLEMAN:
(Whispers to the woman.) A pair of shoe.

WOMAN:
A pair of shoes.

INSPECTOR CHOKO CHOKO:
Now a description of the mob. Can you give me a rough estimate of the crowd?

WOMAN:
The undying roar and numerous, indefatigable footfalls tell of hundreds of people.

INSPECTOR CHOKO CHOKO:
Do they look terribly wild and aggressive?

WOMAN:
God! They are savage beasts! Monsters and vampires! Tigers and bears in human shapes! They carry all sorts of weaponry as though an elephant hunt.

INSPECTOR CHOKO CHOKO:
(Visibly uncomfortable.) Then…then it is a lost case.

WOMAN:
What are you saying officer! You are the police! My son's life is at stake here. He is hardly a man yet and can always grow up to change.

INSPECTOR CHOKO CHOKO:
(Laughs mockingly.) Change indeed! What a sickening familiar refrain! It is an old song!

WOMAN:
Do you have a sense of duty, sir?

INSPECTOR CHOKO CHOKO:
And you, what about your duty as a mother? Did you educate him enough?

WOMAN:
Why not do what ought to be done and save the boy or you will have to answer for it.

INSPECTOR CHOKO CHOKO:
Quiet madame! Shut up! Don't rush me. *(Brief pause.)* Now listen, I really want to help, but I can't.

WOMAN:
But why not, officer? Why not?

INSPECTOR CHOKO CHOKO:
We are just two of us at the station…but that is not even the trouble.

WOMAN:
What is the trouble then?

INSPECTOR CHOKO CHOKO:
The fact is… the police van has been dry for weeks now.

WOMAN:
I beg your pardon!

INSPECTOR CHOKO CHOKO:
I said we have run out of fuel.

WOMAN:
Jesus! The blood of this boy will surely prick our consciences till the end of time.

INSPECTOR CHOKO CHOKO:
(Giggles.) Amen! Amen, madam. Such empty sentimentalities are not hot enough to melt my frozen breast. And what do you expect? I cannot possibly fill up the van with money from my pocket and watch my children perish of hunger. I am a family man. *(Brief pause.)* Look here, I promise to send in a third application to my boss, requesting for a fill-up; who knows, the reply may reach me in a fort-night.

WOMAN:
You cannot be serious. My yard is eaten away by a firestorm of protesters and you tell me to wait!

INSPECTOR CHOKO CHOKO:
Look here, madam, I will not beat about the bush. I don't fabricate petrol. If you badly want your son alive then fill up the tanks and I will do my duty.

WOMAN:
(Almost weeping.) Please do save my son. I will pay for everything; no expense spared.

INSPECTOR CHOKO CHOKO:
O no madame, don't get me wrong. The money is for the fuel – the fuel only. Of course, the government rewards me handsomely for my dutiful services.

WOMAN:
Just be fast about it, sir; there is great need to rush.

INSPECTOR CHOKO CHOKO:
50000 FCFA is the charge. Non-negotiable. Cash in hand.

WOMAN:
It's fine by me, sir. But you must hurry up.

INSPECTOR CHOKO CHOKO:
Good! Where did you say the place is?

WOMAN:
Chief's Street, Buea Town.

INSPECTOR CHOKO CHOKO:
Don't be panicky madam. It is well; you and your son are saved. Dry your tears but remember: cash in hand.

WOMAN:
Cash in hand, sir…make haste…God bless you.
(The woman hangs up. She looks at the gentleman who nervously paces about. During her telephone conversation, he had frequently peeped through the window whenever there was an outcry from the mob outside.) The police is coming.

GENTLEMAN:
(Fretful gestures.) That swine! That devil of an idiot! He spoiled everything! I was getting on well. Shit!

WOMAN:
(Stands up.) Your hands…

GENTLEMAN:
Why not bind the idiot to hell! God!

WOMAN:
…they are like wool.

GENTLEMAN:
That I have to rot in the hands of famished beats! Damn it!

WOMAN:
Your grip was hesitant and weak. Goodness, you are no criminal or robber. Who are y…?

GENTLEMAN:
Good God woman, sit down and shut up! I am trying to think. *(Brief pause. Gazes at the huge portrait on the wall.)* Who is this? Your son?

WOMAN:
He was.

GENTLEMAN:
Born a Cameroonian; served America. Well then, where did he meet his fate? At the sultry desert mountains of Afghanistan or the vast burning sands of Iraq?

WOMAN:
On the cursed, bloodthirsty destitute ground of Bomaka; where babies whined endlessly with bloodsucking teeth; where girls wear used tyres around their necks and boys piss petrol; where the broke hands of men are heavy with blood-stained iron-rods and match-boxes and the cold bitter breasts of women are blackened with frustration and vindictiveness; where God is dead.

GENTLEMAN:
Yours is a very heavy heart, ma'am. Make light your burden, empty your mind.

WOMAN:
My boy was called Emmanuel. His friends nick-named him Pope, seeing that he was highly intelligent. I called him Angel, owing to his loving and caring nature. He never knew his father. I brought him up all by myself. *(Brief pause. Walks to the portrait.)* He could have been a scientific genius. His liking for the sciences knew no bounds. Night and day he talked of Aquatic Biology, Aquatic Biology...How aching, how vexing that our make-shift universities offered no such course! Then he had me worried with this obsession of traveling abroad. He would not lie to rest but go browsing day and night and for days and weeks until he won a scholarship to study Aquatic Biology in the States. He later joined the U.S. Marine.
(She walks away from the portrait.) I had been to the States a countless time, to visit him; and he endeavoured

to come home when he could. *(Sighs.)* The devil! On the 27th of September 2006, he came home never to return. *(sighs.)* The devil! *(Weeps a little.)* The devil! He was only twenty-seven, vigorous, prosperous and promising. His duplex was ready to receive him and he was ready to take a wife. But the devil was at work! *(Brief pause. Walks in circles, rapidly.)* Why did he even come back? Must he come back home for a wife? Was American short of women? Whether black, white, brown or red, did it matter? Are there not Cameroonian women in America? A woman is a woman. Ah! The devil! The devil! And that phone call, why did he answer it? Why did he leave this house? Why didn't he go in his car? Why did he wear a baseball cap, a black shell suit, and a pair of trainers? Why did God make him lean and tall and of ripe banana hue? And what was his business at Bomaka? Why why why? *(She drops into a chair, buries her face in her hands and weeps silently. The gentleman gradually walks towards her, puts out a hand, and then withdraws it.)*

GENTLEMAN:
But…what happened precisely at Bomaka?

WOMAN:
They mistook my son for a thief. A barbershop was robbed of its shaver and the thief had vanished into thin air. But an eyewitness, the boy who had raised the alarm, pointed in the direction of the vanishing thief and gave so deadly a description that fitted my boy. The thief was lean, tall and light. He was in sports-wear. The lynch mob met my boy at the rocky path. Their minds, so crooked and twisted with frustration, helplessness and wickedness did not bring into question the thief's coming towards them instead of running away. All sorts of weapons fell on him. They poured petrol on him and stroke a match. They wouldn't hear from him. *(Sighs.)* The devil! If they

had only given him an ear, he would have invited them to discover his shaving paraphernalia – latest technology – in his bathroom. But o! The famished tigers hastily tore the lamp limb from limb while the hyena scuttled away, a dry bone in fangs, into the arms of freedom. I lost my son in the hands of a lost people.

GENTLEMAN:
How cruel! How barbaric! Be it a thieving of useless peels, chaff or wood-ash, the mob is very much ready to commit the thief to the flames.

WOMAN:
The sun was setting when I received the call. It was my son's number but not his voice. The man said he was a police officer and that they had failed from stopping a mob from burning a thief alive at Bomaka – a thief who may be a relation of mine. I hurried to the scene and saw nothing short of atrocious barbarism! Sheer savagery! Brute bestiality! Could I recognize the boy I had carried in my womb for nine months? *(Sighs. Weeping.)*
There was a heap of sooty ash and some particles of burnt tyre and wires. I strained my eyes and there upon the heap I saw something…all smallish and huddled up like a burnt monkey, its sooty teeth and murky gum hanging on the outside. The flesh was charred and smoky…the bowel had exploded, exposing intestines now twisting like a pack of hungry maggots. The back was bent and red swollen, overfilled blister splitting open to gush smelly blackish, whitish red pus. The air hung with the unbearable, nauseating stench of grilled human meat and baked blood. How disgusting! *(Spits. Stops weeping abruptly, wipes her tears with the back of his hand.)*
I gathered what was left of the remains: picked a finger the stench of scorched hair, a sore toe, a sooty ear, a

cooked tongue, a roasted lip, a baked liver, broiled kidneys – all of these I buried in my yard.

GENTLEMAN:
Oh! Have we become beasts? Is man now a savage bear to tear his kind limp from limp, without fear for man and God? ; to smile and laugh and be at the sight of blackish whitish red blood?

WOMAN:
He had rather died as a hero, gun in hand, fighting for a moral cause than be crushed by beastly hands , lost hands which have bled dry from injustice and now seek to revive their veins with innocent blood. *(She begins to weep again, silently. The gentleman places a hand on her shoulder. She stops weeping. He withdraws his hand.)*

GENTLEMAN:
Some with degrees and high professional skills get themselves into thieving because the government has turned this nation into an unemployment spot. We see the nation's youth, highly educated and vibrant, going to waste on *bend-sekin* and call-boxes. Many have arduously worked their brains into thick and stout muscles only to be obliged to rely on the thin and feeble strength in their arms. Can primary or college drop-outs take on anything when there is hardly any odd job to manage? It is no strange sight to find men and women, thirty and above, with five or six children, living under their old parents' roof, scrambling for food with their own children from their old parents' empty pots. *(Brief pause.)* Others are mere lazybones, yet others can only boast of a blind ambition; dreaming daylong of jet-planes, limousines and villas when their dwarf skills can hardly afford a second-hand spoke. And so, they break into banks and supermarkets to fulfil their unattainable goals. But

ma'am, your son...he was neither one nor the other.
Wherever he is, probably in heaven, he should wear a big
sweet smile on his face for you. It takes a good mother to
raise an upright son. *(Sighs regrettably.)* The kind of
mother I had wished for all my life.

WOMAN:
(Touched by his last words.) But... you are not an orphan,
are you?

GENTLEMAN:
Far from it. I am the unavoidable consequence of a
mother's excesses. She spared the rod and spoiled the
child.

WOMAN:
A mother can only pray and wish the best for her son.

GENTLEMAN:
Well, a mother's overdone and preposterous love for her
devil-son blinds her wholly of his huge horns.

WOMAN:
Bah gentleman, you are unjustly hard on the very poor
woman who without love wouldn't have given you life.

GENTLEMAN:
It is her attitude that is wholly unjustified, completely
unjustifiable. The excessive water of her love had
drowned the flower of my character. It started at a tender
age. My mouth hardly full of teeth, I dipped my filthy tiny
fingers in hot pots and scorching bowls and emptied them
of the meat pieces. What did mother say? She crammed
by bowl full of huge slices of meat by way of remedy.
(Giggles.) How a thief's thirst to reap where he did not
sow is unquenchable! My kid sisters' voices were too

small to have an impact. Any other relative who did as much as to complain about my thieving attitude was sent packing by my lovely mother. Mark you, mother was skilled at inventing. And by some miracle, she always managed to serve father a slice or two of meat at dinner.

WOMAN:
Your mother wasn't certainly the best in that respect, but is it worthy to blame your thieving attitude on some childhood triviality? Who, as a child, was not tempted to open the hot pot?

GENTLEMAN:
Time passed and cursed me with a height, a broken voice and black wires under my armpit and chin. I had also developed the taste and likings that come with liquor and girls. Sure enough, one thing could buy them all – money. Money became my everything: my oxygen, my food, my blood, my life, my water. I was suffocating without money, I always needed money…with money in my pocket, I carried myself about like a king. I started humbly with coins, and mother paid me no heed. Then I graduated to banknotes. Whenever my kid sisters complained, mother was quick to defend and make up for me. She would straighten up and fix them with those fire-burning eyes and then say, "None in the days of my father was a thief; none in my days; none in the billion and billions of years to come. I don't want to hear that! My son is not a thief! My blood is not a thief!" The go ahead was obvious. I didn't sleep. I went grubbing in tresses, under armpits, between legs and in heaving and snoring breasts for a purse.

WOMAN:
Bah! Bah! You hadn't taken it that far.

GENTLEMAN:
I was only a child.

WOMAN:
Well, your mother overstepped the boundaries of her love for you.

GENTLEMAN:
Oh yes, she did. And when I stole 500.000FCFA *njangi-*money from her suit-case, did she report me to the police? *(Giggles.)* She entered into negotiation with me. She will forget about the theft if I return half the money. How she cajoled me! In the end, I handed her one fifth of the sum – after she had had a good long cry. But then, basking in maternal love and protection, I over-stretched my restless hands and they fell on father's wallet. Before I knew it, I was shivering in the cell. But did I learn my lesson? I had barely passed two nights in cell when I was discharged. (Giggles.) Mother would not hear of my detention. She threatened to throw herself into the well. She refused to wash up, refused to cook, refused to eat or drink…she only whined daylong, mourning for a son very much alive. And then I went from bad to worse. My thieving prowess grew another muscle and transgressed our household. In fact, I was cursed! I am cursed!

WOMAN:
A curse? You are only mystifying an ordinary situation that is rectifiable. Goodness knows, what parents would put their child under such a curse?

GENTLEMAN:
The curse came from outside. It came the day I pinched 25FCFA from the table of an orange seller by the Sand-pit road-side. I was dying to smoke. The orange seller came to report me to mother, without any ill-intention, but as

one mother to another for the good of the child. But o, my mother would not hear. She wouldn't take the insult. She bounced on her and insults and punches fell on the poor woman. Before she left, the angry woman vowed that I shall see no light but darkness my whole life. She said, "What is 25FCFA that I am ridiculed by a thieving mother and son? I am stolen and yet beaten. It shall not go unnoticed. The eyes of the stealing hands shall fix on nothing but dry weeds, his hands shall hook only stubbles and chaffs and his legs shall not cease to run after dead leaves and maggots until they fall him down."

WOMAN:
Well, those were harsh words no doubt; but everybody spits fire and vomits storm when they are very angry.

GENTLEMAN:
Except that I had been a thief to no purpose, a fruitless fool, ever since those evil words crossed her lips. Just how many times have I broken into a well-equipped store only to make off with a packet of cigarette or sheath? Did I not witness my neighbour laugh his head off at the idiot of a burglar who had slipped into his off-licence in the dead of the night and had walked away with not more than two bottles of Castel, leaving intact 150000FCFA in the drawer of the counter? I may go from one silly event to another and your ears shall surely sigh of boredom and fatigue. To crown it all, I use to catch myself a many time stealing from myself, pinching and snatching objects I had stolen some time ago. As it is, I am just from stealing a white pair of loafers although I have black and brown ones, sparkling new pairs…all stolen too…but tell me ma'am, you believe a normal thief can act thus?

WOMAN:
I must accept it is strange but …, well, now that you are aware of the evil, what do you intend to do?

GENTLEMAN:
What can I do? What have I not done? Where has mother not taken me to? Priests, pastors, miracle-workers, prophets, soothsayers, witchdoctors, medical-doctors…I have known them all. Just how many times have I collapsed under the power of a sacred ring, confessing my sins in the open and putting the devil to shame? My skin is thoroughly and painfully scarred by medicinal blades. My blood itches and prickles painfully with all sorts of potion and concoctions – yet I would barely tread the saintly path for a fortnight and then derail and plunge back into the dark immoral ways for the rest of the year.

WOMAN:
My goodness! You must have suffered in the hands of charlatans. I have this friend of mine who is privileged to commune with the Almighty…
(There is a loud battering at the gate. Angry protesters demand the thief be handed immediately to them. They menace to break open the gate.)

GENTLEMAN:
(Visibly trembling.) Not like this…I am a man, I am divine…I don't want to die…don't want to die like a dog…they won't burn me to the ground like a mole…no no no…I am a man.. I am divine…sacred…I am sacred….

WOMAN:
(Weepy.) Goodness why! The station is not a long way away, what is taking them so long?

(The uproar from the crowd outside increases. It is obvious that the mob is within the gates, not far from the door.) They must have smashed their way through my gate. I must go to them; I must stop them lest they break open my door. I must go out there and face them.

GENTLEMAN:
(Shaky.) No. Don't ma'am. They…they won't listen to you. You…you can't tame a pack of famished…famished hyenas.

WOMAN:
(Insisting.) It is our only chance. I must distract them with my talk as we wait for the police or let them break down that door and take hold of you.
(The uproar approaches. The woman makes for the door.) You may hide yourself in the wardrobe. *(She places her hand on the knob, takes it off and turns round to face the gentleman.)* Or in the ceiling…

|**GENTLEMAN:**
(Fear has reddened his eyes.) My father….He is a good man. *(Brief pause.)* My mother too. I am a pest.

WOMAN:
It is not true. Your actions are misdirected by an enemy force beyond your control. The curse is the pest.

GENTLEMAN:
Tell them I am sorry …sorry for the pains and shame I caused them.

WOMAN:
But…but I don't even know them.

GENTLEMAN:
They will come to you.
(He walks reluctantly toward the room door, then makes a slight turn and whispers.)
Be careful out there, ma'am.
(He walks to the room. The woman stands by the door in contemplation.) Ma'am?

WOMAN:
Yes.

GENTLEMAN:
My name is DIVINE. *(There is an embarrassing silence.)* Ma'am?

WOMAN:
Yes.

GENTLEMAN:
You are a good woman. Sorry for your son.

WOMAN:
(A moment of silence.) Thank you – DIVINE.
(She opens the door with a new energy and dashes off.)
Blackout

.

FOURTH MOVEMENT

An unruly mob. The demonstrators carry all sorts of weaponry: machetes, hoes, mental rods, axes, sticks, tyres, spades, blades, hammers, nails seven-to-nine inches long, folks, mallet, etc. They clap hands, stamp feet and sing songs as of a hunt; howling the thief be handed without delay to them. The woman emerges from a corner. A man raises his hand and the mob silences.

CRIPPLE:
Whosoever shields a thief surely shall writhe to death under bloody stones. Woman, where is the boy?

WOMAN:
I … I greet you good people…

CRIPPLE:
Keep your greetings to yourself and hand over the boy. Either you join us in our fight or you leave this street. To stand in our way might be very dangerous for you. It is suicide. Now, bring out the boy!

WOMAN:
Madam …you seem a nice woman and…and you are a mother too…

CRIPPLE:
I am neither a woman nor a mother. I have no patience in my heart. You aggravate your case by protecting a thief.

WOMAN:
It is not the boy, it is the curse.

CRIPPLE:
What are you talking about?

WOMAN:
The boy was cursed from childhood. The devil runs in his veins and he can't do anything about it.

CRIPPLE:
The more reason he should be burnt to the ground. He is evil.

WOMAN:
He is not; the curse is evil. The curse should be burnt to the ground. Madam, a gifted man-of –God can release him from the devil's clutches. Good people, killing does not solve the problem; it rather weighs the mind with restlessness and everlasting nightmares. Let us hand the boy to the police and then go for a veritable man-of-God, I beg of you.

HALFARM:
(Cuts in.) The po-what? The police has no business here. *(He presents the stumps of his arms to the woman.)* You see these? They used to be long and taut and solid and amply whole; they use to drive load-jammed Lorries from Garoua to Njamena, from Cameroon to Gabon and Equatorial Guinea; they use to put food on my table and bring sunshine in my household. *(Sighs.)* Not anymore. *(He moves to her so that there is contact – forehead to forehead.)* And do you know why? The police cut them off.

WOMAN:
(Shocked.) The police? They are supposed to protect us, they are our friends…

BLINDMAN:
(Breaks in.) I see that you are not only new around here but ignorant as well. Some of us were born in this street, and others have been living here for over 30 or 40 years and nothing has changed. Ever heard of Ramboman? Of course not. He rendered this street sleepless and restless long before you came here. A most feared criminal of unsurpassed notoriety. We suffered a series of attacks, even in broad daylight, and he made off with our wages and phones. He broke into our houses and our mothers, wives, sisters and daughters were raped; our accessories, clothes, equipment – all gone; our goats, pigs and fowls disappeared - even our dogs and cats. He killed cold-bloodedly who ever dared him. We reported to the police but the police was all lax and reluctant – as though they expected a motivation from us. We pressed on, and one day the police stormed the street but Ramboman kept out of sight. They returned to their station never to show up again despite our protest. Abandoned to ourselves, Pa'a Halfarm and I formed groups and kept a round-the-clock vigil until we seized Ramboman and happily handed him over to the police. How happy we were in our naivety! Barely a week after, we realized our mistake: Ramboman was out of jail and free. He launched an assault against my house and said to me, "I am the filth and the rake; the umpire and the wrestler; the culprit and the judge." And then before I knew it, he thrust a dagger into my eyes.

HALFARM:
He swooped down upon me, swung his vengeful machete and my arms fell off. But then, God nourished our will and strength and when we arrested him for a second time, we burnt his fat black heart to the ground. And then our street could breathe again. But it is true that evil is worse than blood; you can brush and brush but it can never disappear completely; and so, thieves continue to roam

our street day and night. We have equally made it a ritual that every thief or criminal who treads this street shall know no better treatment than to be burnt alive. As for the police, they have no business here.

BLINDMAN:
They grumble at the sight of the poor. They are weak, helpless and not a dime would drop if held upside-down. When thieves broke into my house and I called the police what did they say? *(Mimicking.)* "What do thieves want from a wretched fellow?"

HALFARM:
Neither do they have love for the rich. They are influential and judicially conscious. The police rather dreads them. They have an eye on their pockets though. They may always reap a reward for treating them with honour, respect, adoration and favour.

BLINDMAN:
Theirs is a thieving department. They are quick to hold down a poor fellow, to molest and squeeze the very last coin from him. Once I was locked up and after my bail I walked back home without my phone, cap and watch.

MADWOMAN:
(A doll pressed on her breast. Cuts in.) The police is wicked wicked wicked…they fooled me and let him go unpunished…the spoilt rotten boy crazed with arrogance and sheer obstinacy…he seized his father's jeep and flash past at breakneck speed with shaky legs and unsteady hands…without a licence…with liquor flowing in veins…he speeded through the pot-holed streets as though a corridor in his father's villa…wicked wicked wicked…the jeep roared, and crouched and skidded then it bounced off the road and crushed my son to

death...crushed my boy with four mighty claws...my nine-year-old boy sitting on the pavement...wicked wicked wicked...blood blood blood all over the place...blood blood blood on peeled and unpeeled oranges scattered all over the road...all over the place...wicked wicked wicked...the police came there and snatched the spoilt rotten boy from the violent hands of the wild crowd...wicked wicked wicked police... they promised to throw him in prison for life but rather threw him into the very first plane making for the States...wicked wicked police...my son is cold cold underground selling oranges all alone without a mother but not the spoilt rotten murderer...he is feasting with his mother abroad every blessed day...O wicked wicked police ...take me to my son ...wicked wicked police...bring back my son... *(Starts weeping bitterly. Some men go to console her.)*

CRIPPLE:
(With venom.) Enough of this rubbish! We are only wasting time. Drag that robber out here before he slips away.

WOMAN:
(Softly.) Eh madam, you seem a nice person....You are reasonable enough to avoid taking the law into your hands. Please, give the boy a chance to mend his ways. He is only in his mid-twenties. The jail will certainly set him straight again.

CRIPPLE:
It is even precautionary to wring the neck of a fledging chick before it grows lengthy razor-sharp claws and preys on the world. Who is not aware that the jam-packed prisons are no rehabilitation centres! They cannot restore the boy his moral sense; rather, they turn jackals into

hyenas and make crocodiles of lizards. We shall extirpate them all even before they grow a wing or leave their nests.

WOMAN:
But madam, it cannot be overemphasized that the International Human Rights Law condemns the violation of a person's right to be innocent until proven guilty.

CRIPPLE:
(Giggles.) Is that so? Who is innocent here? We caught the boy red-handed trying to play on an old man's intelligence and walk away with goods and money.

WOMAN:
It is only less prejudicial to mistakenly spare a culprit than hang an innocent. It is too regrettable and appalling to be a law unto yourself and break with the laws of man and God. You break these laws in a desperate bid to punish the law-breakers. Is one law-breaker worthy to punish another?

CRIPPLE:
The Lord shall not cease to nourish my will and I will make it a duty to stamp the devil out of this street. Put every evil-doer, a foetus or a dying hag, to extirpation. Our street shall be evil-free. As for the law of man, it is meaningless; it is stuck in the tongues of men and not in their hands. I will go my own way. I will add my own rules to the law and above all give it life.

WOMAN:
But ...all this is far from being fair. God is up high watching.

CRIPPLE:
He cannot do it for us; we must fight for ourselves. We don't want to be fair; we only fight for survival. Can you talk of fairness when one is shorn of the blooms and bliss of life at a flowering age? Or you think I had crept on my bottom all my life! I too had been a woman, a beauty for that matter. Tall and straight as a palm tree, horsey in hip, graceful in limb, light of foot, with soft springy steps of a deer, thighs like a moving piston, nails like pieces of shiny mirrors…and yes, my head was always high in the sky because I was aware of my beauty. My word was a law among the men folk. So, I picked amongst them the one with the heaviest pocket. But we had hardly tasted the sweetness of life when armed burglars stumped into our house. My stubborn husband! He would not disclose the code of his coffers until the red-eye gang leader chopped off my legs, one after the other. Finally, the gang made off with fifteen million FCFA. We fell from grace to disgrace. My husband took to the bottle and made the red-light district his new home. Eventually I became unattractive, unthought-of and unattended to; for what can attract a man to a grotesque creature that drags itself daylong like a crawling viper?

BITTERMAN:
(He walks to the woman as though to assault her. Cuts in.) What is fair in being brutally cut off from one's hard-earned happiness? *(Faces the audience.)* We were about to consume our marriage when the door banged open and the villains invaded our bridal bed. I wept loud and long like a hungry child whose meat was about to be snatched by a bully. But… where was the police? *(Shrugs.)* They ran off with our wedding clothes, our wedding rings and our wedding presents and they won't end there… *(Sobs.)* Oh! My virgin wife! My patience and her preservation had come to nothing! Nothing! They ruined her vows of

chastity! The beasts! Where was the police? They took turns on her! Where was the police? So vigorously and violently they were bouncing and striking and hammering as though their aim was to maim her, to destroy her, to render her lifeless....blood blood everywhere. Where was the police? They were chopping and crushing as of a sharpened and heavy hatchet on a fragile daffodil. They crushed her into unconsciousness and all the time they obliged me to watch the scene, my hands and legs tied together. Where was the police? The police came as usual when the dust had settled and they promised to arrest the criminals yet the issue has been under investigation for thirty-four years now and nothing has come out of it. The officers who started the investigation are retired now, some are dead and the new ones seem to know nothing about the incident. The file is missing. *(Brief pause. He weeps for a while.)* Thereafter, my wife was never the same again. My love, tenderness, patience and understanding were not enough to heal her shattered mind. She lost her life in an abortion. Thieves, burglars, robbers, rapists, police, politicians – I put them all in a basket. I have nothing for them but death.

BASTARD:
Is it fair to be sentenced and rejected because of the crimes of another? From the day I was born, eyes have been glaring at me, fingers pointing at me, and tongues sighing, curling and cursing me, "A cobra's semen carry no lamb; a cobra's semen full of spittle" My mother too, of all, glared and pointed in her own way. She would beat me hard and long for a broken glass as though I had set the house on fire. Then one day I looked around me and asked the most dreaded question, "Mother, where is my father?" The response was immediate and harsh. Mother beat me like a snake. She lashed me unconscious. I groaned and whined while she whipped and wept, then I

cried no more. I had understood without her explaining. She does not know my father; I am the lasting memorial of a despicable incident, a regrettable and most detestable momento. But…is it my fault? *(Brief pause as though he waits for the answer.)* With time things went from bad to worse. Eyes glared, fingers pointed, and mouths curled. On seeing me, men would feel for their wallets, women would hold tightly on to their handbags, and girls gazed with frightful, watchful eyes as if I were some aliens from space. And so, I left everything behind me and went to a foreign land, where I was a stranger. But can you run away from your memories? It is like trying to run away from your shadow. It comes and goes with the sun. I would begin to relish the peace and bliss meant for strangers when suddenly I would be woken from my sweet dream by an angry mob lynching a thief; and I would be invited to join in the struggle. Then my tranquillity would be ruined by the heinous image of an unknown villainous father resurfacing to torture my sick mind. It is a small world we live in. Other times I would run into an old face of the past and then the eyes would begin to glare, the fingers point and the mouth curl and curse. And so, I am always on the run, running away from glaring eyes, accusing fingers and cursing tongues…. And this has made me to be bitter, so that every time a thief or a rapist is caught, I beat and torture him as though I were revenging against my father.

WOMAN:
Yes… I understand what you've been through and … and I …I see a cause for your wrath …I have also lost a son unjustly but I don't think the right way is to revenge. See, I have been talking with the boy and I swear he is no rapist, he cannot harm a fly…he is only a petty thief, a rogue…

CRIPPLE:
We can never be too sure about that. For all I know, a thief rapes his victim one way or the other. Thieves have become worse than rapists and killers. In fact, it is uncommon to see a thief who is not a rapist and a killer. They steal money, goods and kidnap human beings; kill them and butchered off vital body parts and organs to sell off: nipples, clitoris, testicles, penises, umbilical cords, kidneys, livers, bladders, brains – all of these are sold to vampire politicians who are crazed with immortality, necromantic business giants and haunted wealthy persons.

WOMAN:
It's obvious: the earth is certainly crumbling. But to meet storm with storm will not save the situation.

CRIPPLE:
(Bitterly.) I would set the earth on fire or floods were they in my power.

WOMAN:
My heart is also heavy and bitter, yet I maintain that killing is no solution to thieving. The one has not only failed to overcome the other but it has created angry and vengeful minds between the mass and thieves.

CRIPPLE:
There is no better alternative.

WOMAN:
We should report and leave all criminal cases in the hands of experts on criminal law.

CRIPPLE:
And who do you refer to as experts?

WOMAN:
The police and the courts.

CRIPPLE:
There you go again. I see it's pointless talking with you. *(To the mob.)* Gentlemen, time calls for action. Let's tear down the nest and snatch life out of the eaglet. Be quick and hard to crush every soul in your way. Who would flap protective wings over the eaglet if not the eagle? Go and drag the hatchling here! Go! The flames are hungry.
(The mob marches towards the woman's house, singing.)

WOMAN:
(She stands in their way – pleading.) Please, hear me out good people. *(The men hesitate.)*

CRIPPLE:
(Angrily.) What is this! Have men become weaklings? Or you have changed masters? Get her, bundle her up! Tie her up! Quick!
(Two men get hold of the woman. Her effort to break free is fruitless. They carry her off stage. Except for the cripple, the blind-man and the half-arm, the mob stomps angrily off stage – shouting and cheering. We hear the sound of a broken door, the stamping of feet, the clink clank of metals, roaring voices, a scream and a struggle. The mob re-emerges with a bundle on its head and flings it onto the ground. The gentleman wriggles under kicks and blows. The mob moves in on him so that we cannot see him anymore; we only hear his agonized cry beneath the heavy blows which are uninterrupted by the fading light. Darkness comes and there is a sudden burst of flames. Voices cheer, feet stamp and then quieten. A dim light gradually lightens the empty stage, the middle of which bears a smouldering bundle: a charred, smoky carcass. A passer-by approaches.)

PASSER-BY:
(Wrinkles his nose in disgust.) I witnessed it all today: man can only be man by biology and physique; but man can be anything –beasts, monster, saint or god – by reason and psychology.
I saw men with human legs and zombie heads in a stifling and unliveable atmosphere. I saw men vomit the emptiness of their black infested hearts. I saw man aimed his righteous lance at the wrong target in a bid to right the impropriety of unreliable, venal police officers and the indolence of a slow-footed, wrong-rated judiciary which have shattered every beauty, satisfaction and compensation that spring from justice. I saw men trapped in a pit void of the oxygen of justice and choking in the thick fumes of injustice. I saw the hungry eyes of men: hungry for justice and above all loomed the hunger of hungers, the biggest and cruellest of all, that which detaches the soul from the body, that which keeps the stomach grumbling. The mob is young and ambitious, yet idle. Eager and youthful hands set to work: they dig down deep into the earth of our forefathers for a job as much as the pig for the mythical stone. Unemployment can only foment hunger and hunger surely stirs the embers of anger. A famished, growling stomach is earless; it can only be harsh, hasty, cruel, riotous, rampageous, wild, raging, rancorous…
(A noise off stage. The passer-by moves to a dim corner. Two officers enter stage. They cover their noses with their hands, looking at the smouldering carcass with dark staring eyes.)

FIRST OFFICER:
Shit! Once again, we are too late.

SECOND OFFICER:
(Eating boiled groundnut in a greedy manner.) I won't say we didn't try our best.

FIRST OFFICER:
I cannot afford to ignore this lax and nonchalant attitude of ours.

SECOND OFFICER:
Relax man; it is not the end of the world. Who knows what fire could have been vomited by that volcano of a crazed mob? It is always better to come after the storm, man. Why do you think inspector Choko Choko is not with us? *(Chews energetically.)*

FIRST OFFICER:
Shit! The bloodletting beasts would rather roast a man faster than a goat. All this for a petty pair of shoes.

SECOND OFFICER:
I won't say we are not trying tooth and nail; but two officers against a hundred or so savage people is no easy case, man. *(Throws a handful of groundnuts in his mouth.)*

FIRST OFFICER:
Now the place is a grave; a dark hostile silence. Murderers have crept away to their houses without leaving as much as a footprint.
(The passer-by walks pass them, in a hurry.)
Mister? *(The passer-by does not respond.)* Sir?

SECOND OFFICER:
Hey, you there! Stop there! *(The passer-by stands still, frightened.)* Come here! *(He walks timidly to the officers.)* You should be one of them.

PASSER-BY:
(Confused and terrified.) Yes Chef, no Chef… I …I don't leave here…I am just passing…

FIRST OFFICER:
Fear not gentleman. We just wish to hear from an eye-witness. Where you present at the start? Can you tell us what happened?

PASSER-BY:
I will try, Chef.

SECOND OFFICER:
Well, we are listening. *(He has finished eating so that he uses his fingers to pick bits of food from between his teeth and cleans his hands on his uniform.))*

PASSER-BY:
When I heard the uproar, I hastened to the scene. The mob already had the thief clawed down like a gazelle in a lion's fangs. They stripped him naked; they pounded him with sticks and stones and all sorts of rods. Kicks and slaps and punches and knees and elbows landed on every fibre of his body. He was like a man caught in a collapsed house. The poor helpless creature wriggled and whined in pain and agony like a worm in live coals. He screamed and wailed and then lost his voice in the process: no matter how long and wide he opened his mouth not a syllable was uttered except the heavy flow of blood. It gushed from every possible opening: eyes, ears, nostrils, mouth, anus, urethra – even the pores were red wet. I thought it over when his legs gave out and he collapsed. But to my dismay, they brought a glass bottle charged with super-heated bubbly water and with it brutally and wholly massaged him to the bone. The poor creature

screamed, struggled, jerked and then plunged into convulsions. The thick fleshy skin was falling out leaving deep open red sores and swellings. Before long, violent hands raised him to his staggering feet. A seven-to-nine long inches nail and a gigantic hammer came to light. The nail was set on his scalp and the hammer lifted up. When it came down, the scream was deafening, blood pumped out as though a tap was turned on, and thick lines zigzagged on the scalp like an earth under a violent quake. He passed out once again. But the mob could not be contented with flogging a dead horse. They spilled some strong smelly liquid on the thief's bloody face and he sprang back to life; started a battle: an over-determined, combative spirit struggling against a weary, dying body. He ventured a futile escape and the mob mocked him by giving him a chance that fits that given by a cat to a blind, limping rat. Whether in lack of terror-giving instruments or short of ferocious forms of torture; Whether bursting with their fill or bent to denying the police a half chance – they hastily wore the thief a tyre around his neck, piled wood on him, poured a litre of petrol on him and stroke a match. He went ablaze. His fight against fire was futile: the more he twisted, wriggled, writhed and rolled about the faster he was consumed. Even so, he would battle to his last breath. Some organs deep inside him exploded and the people cheered with relief and they only retired to their houses when the thief was dead and still.

FIRST OFFICER:
(Shocked.) Verily verily God is dead here below. Dead and buried! The devil has taken over.

SECOND OFFICER:
(Cold. It is routine.) Tell me: where does the victim live? What about his mother?

PASSER-BY:
You mean the woman who was bundled up? They are not related. Just some poor woman who sought to save the boy.

SECOND OFFICER:
(Surprised.) You don't mean it? And she is willing to give away fifty thousand FCFA just like that? Are you sure there is nothing between the two?

PASSER-BY:
Well, I cannot say...all I know is that the woman had suffered a bitter experience about mob lynching and she had always stood against it.

SECOND OFFICER:
Now, where is she?

PASSER-BY:
She was rushed to Mount Mary Hospital after she collapsed.

SECOND OFFICER:
Shit! Bullshit! *(To himself.)* What do I do now?

FIRST OFFICER:
(To the passer-by.) Thanks for your time. *(The passer-by hurries off.)*

SECOND OFFICER:
Man, we should rush to Mount Mary for the cash.

FIRST OFFICER:
(Terribly shocked.) Are you deaf or what! The woman is not well.

SECOND OFFICER:
So what! The boss will not have that. What do we do now?

FIRST OFFICER:
Go back and tell him we were late.

SECOND OFFICER:
What if he reminds us that we had left early enough?

FIRST OFFICER:
Tell him we had made three unnecessary stops to check on your numerous *ashawos*.

SECOND OFFICER:
Hold it there man! We are knee-deep in this matter both of us…. Fifty thousand cash! No! The boss won't hear of it! He will be mad! *(His cell phone rings.)* Oh! It is him…it's the boss! What do I tell him?

FIRST OFFICER:
The truth.

SECOND OFFICER:
(Answers the call.) Hello sir, yes sir….I mean no sir. We were not lucky sir…we…the mob gave us no time sir. *(listens for a while.)* Mount Mary Hospital sir. Yes sir. We must collect the money today, sir…I promise. We cannot afford to joke, sir. We are heading there right away, sir. Yes sir. Understood sir. *(The call ends. He breathes hard.)*

FIRST OFFICER:
The truth shall set you free.

SECOND OFFICER:
The Chief Inspector says we must collect the cash from… *(The cell phone rings again. He picks it up.)* Hello sir. *(Listens.)* What! Another thief caught at Muea? *(Listens.)* How much? Yes sir.
Wait a minute. *(To the first officer.)* A pen and paper. *(The first officer pulls a pen and paper from his chest pocket and is ready to write.)* Give the number, sir. 676666666. I have it sir. *(Listens.)* Yes sir. So, I should go to Muea and officer Ngobohstrong should go to Mount Mary and collect your money. It is clear sir. *(The call ends. To first officer.)* The boss says you must go to Mount…

FIRST OFFICER:
(Cuts in.) I am not going to Mount Mary…I have had enough of this shit!

SECOND OFFICER:
It is an order! A command! The inspector is not asking you; he is telling you! Do you want to be sacked from the police?

FIRST OFFICER:
I say I am not going to Mount Mary, and henceforth I will not do this dirty job for the boss. Not anymore! He will dirty his hands himself. I am sick and tired of this treachery and manipulations! I joined this corps to serve and not to exploit and extort.

SECOND OFFICER:
Ok! Alright, I have no time for your philosophy. You will say one thing and do another. *(He begins to go off stage.)*

FIRST OFFICER:
(Follows him.) You will see. I have never disobeyed him but it begins today. I will not put his evil commands to execution just because he is my boss. There must be a way to fight him. I am not going to Mount Mary to extort a poor woman; I will rather go with you to Muea and fight tooth and nail to save the thief from the hands of the lynching mob. *(He follows his colleague with confidence and determination.)*

Blackout

www.ingramcontent.com/pod-product-compliance
Lightning Source LLC
Chambersburg PA
CBHW051705090426
42736CB00013B/2546